No Backbone!
The World of Invertebrates

Spooky Wolf Spiders

by Meish Goldish

Consultant: Brian V. Brown
Curator, Entomology Section
Natural History Museum of Los Angeles County

BEARPORT
PUBLISHING

NEW YORK, NEW YORK

Credits

Cover, © Pascal Goetgheluck/Ardea; 5, © sdewdney/Istockphoto.com; 6T, © Konstantin Kikvidze/Shutterstock; 6C, © Greg Harold/Auscape/Minden Pictures; 6B, © Gary Meszaros/Photo Researchers, Inc.; 7, © Pascal Goetgheluck/Ardea; 8, © Cathy Keifer/Shutterstock; 9, © Cathy Keifer/Shutterstock; 10, © Cathy Keifer/Shutterstock; 11, © Frank Siteman/age fotostock / SuperStock; 12, © Anthony Bannister/Photo Researchers, Inc.; 13, © Jose B. Ruiz/Nature Picture Library/Alamy; 14T, © Graphic Science/Alamy; 14C, © Damian Herde/Shutterstock; 14B, © Bonneau Stéphan/Biosphoto/Peter Arnold Inc.; 15, © Gary Meszaros/Visuals Unlimited; 16, © Dwight Kuhn/Dwight Kuhn Photography; 17, Greg Harold/Auscape/Minden Pictures; 18T, © Dwight Kuhn/Dwight Kuhn Photography; 18B, © Hans Pfletschinger/Peter Arnold; 19, © WildPictures / Alamy; 21, © Oxford Scientific Films/Photolibrary; 22TL, © David Cappaert, Michigan State University, United States; 22TR, © David Kuhn/Dwight Kuhn Photography; 22BL, © Joseph Berger/Bugwood.org; 22BR, © David Kuhn/Dwight Kuhn Photography; 23TL, © Jim Wehtje/Photodisc Green/Getty Images; 23TR, © Dwight Kuhn/Dwight Kuhn Photography; 23BL, © Anthony Bannister/Photo Researchers, Inc.; 23BR, © Cathy Keifer/Shutterstock; 24, © Cathy Keifer/Shutterstock.

Publisher: Kenn Goin *2·24·09*
Editorial Director: Adam Siegel
Creative Director: Spencer Brinker
Design: Dawn Beard Creative
Photo Researcher: James O'Connor

Library of Congress Cataloging-in-Publication Data

Goldish, Meish.
 Spooky wolf spiders / by Meish Goldish.
     p. cm. — (No backbone! The world of invertebrates)
 Includes bibliographical references and index.
 ISBN-13: 978-1-59716-706-2 (library binding)
 ISBN-10: 1-59716-706-1 (library binding)
 1. Wolf spiders—Juvenile literature. I. Title.

 QL458.42.L9G65 2009
 595.4'4—dc22

                              2008006170

For more information, write to Bearport Publishing Company, Inc., 101 Fifth Avenue, Suite 6R, New York, New York 10003. Printed in the United States of America.

10 9 8 7 6 5 4 3 2 1

Contents

Spooky Spiders. 4

Many Kinds, Many Places. 6

Eight Legs, Eight Eyes 8

Hairy Hunters. 10

A Juicy Meal. 12

Staying Safe. 14

Spinning Silk 16

Baby Spiders. 18

Growing Up 20

A World of Invertebrates. 22

Glossary 23

Index 24

Read More 24

Learn More Online 24

About the Author 24

Spooky Spiders

Wolf **spiders** have hairy bodies.

They look spooky, but they are not dangerous to people.

A wolf spider's bite cannot kill a person.

Insects, however, need to watch out.

Wolf spiders are very good at catching and killing them!

Wolf spiders hunt alone. They may have gotten their name because people once thought they hunted in groups, like wolves.

Many Kinds, Many Places

There are more than 2,000 kinds of wolf spiders.

These little creatures live in almost every part of the world.

They are found in both hot and cold places.

They make their homes in forests and deserts, and on beaches and mountains.

Wolf spiders are also found in people's homes and yards.

Some wolf spiders are as small as .2 inches (.5 cm) long. Others can be as big as 2 inches (5 cm).

Eight Legs, Eight Eyes

Wolf spiders have eight legs and eight eyes.

They use their legs to move quickly.

They can use their eyes to look left, right, up, and straight ahead—all at the same time!

Their great speed and sharp eyesight help them catch all kinds of insects.

eyes

eyes

The hairs on a wolf spider's body help it sense things. These hairs can feel movement in the air and on the ground. They can also sense changes in temperature.

legs

legs

legs

Hairy Hunters

Many kinds of spiders spin silk webs to trap their food.

However, wolf spiders catch their food in a different way—they hunt.

A wolf spider waits until it spots an insect that it wants to eat.

Then the hairy hunter suddenly attacks.

Flies, beetles, and crickets are some of the insects that wolf spiders hunt.

fly

10

11

A Juicy Meal

When hunting, a wolf spider quickly runs up to its victim.

Next, it jumps on the insect and bites it with its deadly **fangs**.

The spider also spits juices from its stomach onto the insect.

These juices turn the insides of the insect into a liquid.

The spider's stomach acts like a pump to help it suck up its liquid meal.

A spider uses its fangs to poison an insect. The spider's poison keeps its victim from moving.

fangs

grasshopper

13

Staying Safe

Wolf spiders are fierce hunters, but they also have enemies of their own.

Luckily, the colors of their bodies make them hard to see.

Wolf spiders are brown or gray.

These colors let them blend in easily with rocks, sand, leaves, and trees.

toad

wolf spider

Birds, snakes, frogs, and toads are some of the animals that hunt and eat wolf spiders.

15

Spinning Silk

Like all spiders, wolf spiders use tiny tubes in their bodies to make silk threads.

Wolf spiders don't use their silk to make webs, but they do use it in other ways.

Many kinds dig holes, called burrows, in the ground.

These wolf spiders use silk threads to line the walls of their underground homes.

Also, all female spiders make bags of silk, called **egg sacs**, to protect their eggs.

egg sac

burrow

Not all wolf spiders dig burrows to use as homes. Some live under rocks or in trees. Others just wander from place to place.

Baby Spiders

A female wolf spider lays about 100 eggs at a time.

She wraps them in her egg sac to keep them safe.

When the eggs hatch, the mother spider bites the sac open.

Small spiders, called spiderlings, crawl out of the sac and climb onto her back.

Some kinds of wolf spiders carry around their egg sacs until the eggs hatch. Other kinds keep the sacs in their burrows.

egg sac

spiderlings

spiderlings

Growing Up

Baby wolf spiders stay on their mother's back for about a week.

Then they go off on their own.

As they grow, they shed their hard covering, called an exoskeleton, and grow a new one.

This change, called molting, happens several times.

After the last molt, the spooky-looking spiders are adults—ready to surprise their next victim.

Male wolf spiders live for about a year. Females live for two or three years.

An animal that has a skeleton with a **backbone** inside its body is a *vertebrate* (VUR-tuh-brit). Mammals, birds, fish, reptiles, and amphibians are all vertebrates.

An animal that does not have a skeleton with a backbone inside its body is an *invertebrate* (in-VUR-tuh-brit). More than 95 percent of all kinds of animals on Earth are invertebrates.

Some invertebrates, such as insects and spiders, have hard skeletons—called exoskeletons—on the outside of their bodies. Other invertebrates, such as worms and jellyfish, have soft, squishy bodies with no exoskeletons to protect them.

Here are four spiders that are closely related to wolf spiders. Like all spiders, they are invertebrates.

Fishing Spider

Nursery Web Spider

Yellow Sac Spider

Green Lynx Spider

Glossary

backbone
(BAK-*bohn*)
a group of connected bones that run along the backs of some animals, such as dogs, cats, and fish; also called a spine

egg sacs
(EG SAKS)
the silk containers that female wolf spiders make to protect their eggs

fangs
(FANGZ)
long pointy teeth

spiders
(SPYE-durz)
small animals that have eight legs, two main body parts, and a hard covering called an exoskeleton

Index

backbone 22

burrows 16–17, 18

egg sac 16, 18

eggs 16, 18

enemies 14–15

exoskeleton 20, 22

eyes 8

fangs 12

fishing spider 22

food 10, 12

green lynx spider 22

hair 4, 8, 10

hiding 14

homes 6, 16–17

hunting 4, 8, 10, 12, 14

legs 8–9

life cycle 18, 20–21

molting 20

nursery web spider 22

silk 10, 16

size 7

spiderlings 18–19, 20

webs 10, 16

yellow sac spider 22

Read More

Cooper, Jason. *Wolf Spiders.* Vero Beach, FL: Rourke Publishing (2006).

Murray, Julie. *Wolf Spiders.* Edina, MN: ABDO Publishing (2005).

Learn More Online

To learn more about wolf spiders, visit

www.bearportpublishing.com/NoBackbone-Spiders

About the Author

Meish Goldish has written more than 100 books for children. He lives in Brooklyn, New York, where wolf spiders sometimes visit his home.